# WORKBOOK

## for

# FRENCH VERBS made *EASY* plus

## Rosemary Pitts, M.A.

First Edition August 2021

© 2021 Rosemary Pitts

**2**

These practice sentences are designed to help you master the verbs laid out in "French Verbs Made Easy Plus" (third edition, 2021) by using them to translate simple short phrases.

The verbs are systematically used in the order found in FVMEplus.

So the best way to work is to open FVME at the page referred to and then attempt translating English to French and vice versa.

You could start by covering the answers, and when you have tried your best, check them.

The everyday vocabulary used should help to fix it into your mind.  As you will mostly need to talk about yourself, the **je** form is used.  Later on, it's easy to move on to **tu**, **il/elle**, etc.

Page numbers on the left refer to the VERBS in FVMEplus.

Page numbers on the **right** refer to useful **grammar & vocabulary** information in FVMEplus.

# L'indicatif présent **Pages 6-25**

Use the Present Tense for: what <u>you are doing now</u> or
what <u>you usually do</u>

## -er verbs

| | | | | |
|---|---|---|---|---|
| p.8 | 1 | | je | parle anglais et français |
| p.9 | 2 | | j' | aime la musique et la lecture <sup>reading</sup> |
| p.10 | 3 | | j' | aide <sup>help</sup> mes parents |
| p.10 | 4 | | j' | arrive au collège |
| p.10 | 5 | | je | chante une chanson <sup>song</sup> |
| p.10 | 6 | | je | cherche <sup>look for/search for</sup> mes clefs <sup>keys</sup> |
| p.10 | 7 | | je | commence mes devoirs <sup>homework</sup> |
| p.10 | 8 | | je | dépense <sup>spend</sup> mon argent <sup>money</sup> |
| p.10 | 9 | | je | dessine une poupée <sup>doll</sup> / une auto <sup>car</sup> |
| p.10 | 10 | | je | discute <sup>argue</sup> avec mes sœurs <sup>sisters</sup> |
| p.10 | 11 | | j' | écoute la radio |
| p.10 | 12 | | j' | explique <sup>explain</sup> le problème |
| p.10 | 13 | | je | ferme la fenêtre <sup>window</sup> |
| p.10 | 14 | | je | gagne de l'argent <sup>money</sup> |
| p.11 | 15 | | j' | habite à Londres / Edimbourg |
| p.11 | 16 | | j' | invite mes copains |
| p.11 | 17 | | je | joue au tennis |

# 5

## Present Tense  Pages 6-25

Use the Present Tense for:    what <u>you are doing now</u> or
what <u>you usually do</u>

### -er verbs

| 1 | I speak English and French | |
|---|---|---|
| 2 | I like music and reading | |
| 3 | I help my parents | p.55 |
| 4 | I arrive at school | p.64 |
| 5 | I sing a song | |
| 6 | I look for my keys | p.91/ p.55 |
| 7 | I begin my homework | p.55 |
| 8 | I spend my money | p.55/ p.105 |
| 9 | I draw a doll / a car | |
| 10 | I argue with my sisters | p.55 |
| 11 | I listen to the radio | p.91 |
| 12 | I explain the problem | |
| 13 | I shut the window | |
| 14 | I earn (some) money | p.105/ p.67 |
| 15 | I live in London / Edinburgh | p.99 |
| 16 | I invite my friends | p.55 |
| 17 | I play tennis | p.102 |

| | | | |
|---|---|---|---|
| p.11 | 18 | je | mange un sandwich |
| p.11 | 19 | je | monte go up à ma chambre bedroom |
| p.11 | 20 | je | nage swim à la piscine |
| p.11 | 21 | je | parle speak à mes amis |
| p.11 | 22 | je | pense que c'est magnifique |
| p.11 | 23 | je | porte wear un jean |
| p.11 | 24 | je | pousse push la porte |
| p.11 | 25 | je | prépare un pique-nique |
| p.11 | 26 | je | quitte leave la maison |
| p.11 | 27 | je | raconte tell une histoire story |
| p.11 | 28 | je | regarde la télé |
| p.11 | 29 | je | remercie thank mon père |
| p.11 | 30 | je | reste stay à la maison |
| p.11 | 31 | je | téléphone à mes copains(m)/copines(f) friends |
| p.11 | 32 | je | travaille work dur |
| p.11 | 33 | je | traverse cross la rue |
| p.11 | 34 | je | trouve find mes livres |
| p.11 | 35 | je | voyage en Europe |

You can easily change all of these to
il = he, elle = she, on = one/we

| 18 | I eat a sandwich | |
| --- | --- | --- |
| 19 | I go up to my bedroom | p.55 |
| 20 | I swim at the swimming pool | p.64 |
| 21 | I speak to my friends | p.55 |
| 22 | I think that it's great | p.59 |
| 23 | I wear (a pair of) jeans | |
| 24 | I push the door | |
| 25 | I prepare a picnic | |
| 26 | I leave the house | p.108 |
| 27 | I tell a story | |
| 28 | I watch tv | p.91 |
| 29 | I thank my father | p.55 |
| 30 | I stay at home | p.64 |
| 31 | I phone my friends | p.55 |
| 32 | I work hard | |
| 33 | I cross the road | |
| 34 | I find my books | p.55 |
| 35 | I travel in Europe | p.100 |

You can easily change all of these to
**il** = he, **elle** = she, **on** = one/we

## -ir verbs

| p.12 | 36 | je | finis mes devoirs <sup>homework</sup> |
| p.12 | 37 | je | saisis <sup>grab/seize</sup> mon sac à dos <sup>backpack</sup> |
| p.12 | 38 | je | choisis <sup>choose</sup> un gâteau <sup>cake</sup> |
| p.12 | 39 | je | réfléchis <sup>think/reflect</sup> un moment |
| p.12 | 40 | je | remplis <sup>fill</sup> ma trousse <sup>pencil-case</sup> |

## -re verbs

| p.13 | 41 | j' | attends <sup>wait for</sup> l'autobus |
| p.13 | 42 | j' | entends <sup>hear</sup> un bruit <sup>noise</sup> |
| p.13 | 43 | je | m'entends bien avec <sup>get on well with</sup> mes parents |
| p.13 | 44 | je | réponds à <sup>answer/respond to</sup> la question |

## Slightly irregular -er verbs

| p.14 | 45 | je | m'appelle Louise/Pierre |
| p.16 | 46 | j' | achète <sup>buy</sup> des cds |
| p.16 | 47 | je | me lève <sup>get up</sup> à 6 heures |
| p.16 | 48 | je | me promène <sup>go for a walk</sup> dans le parc |
| p.16 | 49 | j' | espère <sup>hope</sup> aller aux Etats-Unis <sup>USA</sup> |
| p.16 | 50 | je | préfère la campagne <sup>countryside</sup> |

## -ir verbs

| 36 | I finish my homework | p.55 |
|---|---|---|
| 37 | I grab my backpack | p.55 |
| 38 | I choose a cake | |
| 39 | I think for a moment | |
| 40 | I fill my pencil-case | p.55 |

## -re verbs

| 41 | I wait for the bus | p.91 |
|---|---|---|
| 42 | I hear a noise | |
| 43 | I get on well with my parents | p.25/ p.55 |
| 44 | I answer the question | |

## Slightly irregular -er verbs

| 45 | My name is Louise/Peter | p.25/ p.14 |
|---|---|---|
| 46 | I buy (some) CDs | p.16/ p.67 |
| 47 | I get up at 6 o'clock | p.16/ 25/96 |
| 48 | I walk in the park | p.16/ p.25 |
| 49 | I hope to go to the USA | p.16/ p.101 |
| 50 | I prefer the countryside | p.16 |

## Irregular Verbs

| | | | |
|---|---|---|---|
| p.19 | 51 | j' | ai quatorze [14] /quinze [15] /seize [16] ans [years old] |
| p.19 | 52 | je | suis [am] assez [quite] grand(e) [tall] |
| p.19 | 53 | je | vais [go] à l'école à pied [on foot] |
| p.19 | 54 | je | bois [drink] du café |
| p.20 | 55 | je | dois [have to] faire [do] mes devoirs [homework] |
| p.21 | 56 | j' | écris [write] une lettre |
| p.21 | 57 | je | fais [do (go)] du jogging |
| p.22 | 58 | je | mets [put on] mon pull bleu |
| p.22 | 59 | j' | ouvre [open] la porte [door] |
| p.22 | 60 | je | peux [can] sortir [go out] le samedi [on Saturdays] |
| p.22 | 61 | je | prends [take] mon stylo [pen] |
| p.22 | 62 | je | prends [have] un chocolat chaud |
| p.22 | 63 | je | prends [catch] le train |
| p.23 | 64 | je | reçois [receive/get] de l'argent de poche [pocket money] |
| p.23 | 65 | je | ne sais pas [don't know] |

## 11

## Irregular Verbs

| 51 | I am 14/15/16 | p.86/ p.92 |
|---|---|---|
| 52 | I am quite tall | |
| 53 | I walk to school | p.64/ p.107 |
| 54 | I drink some coffee | p.67 |
| 55 | I must/have to do my homework | p.55 |
| 56 | I write a letter | |
| 57 | I go jogging | p.102 |
| 58 | I put my blue pullover on | p.69/ p.70 |
| 59 | I open the door | p.94 |
| 60 | I can go out on Saturdays | p.23/ p.94 |
| 61 | I take my pen | p.55 |
| 62 | I have a hot chocolate | |
| 63 | I catch the train | |
| 64 | I get (some) pocket money | p.67/ p.105 |
| 65 | I don't know | p.48 |

| p.23 | 66 | je | sors <sup>go out</sup> le weekend |
|---|---|---|---|
| p.23 | 67 | je | pars <sup>leave/depart</sup> à 7 heures et demie <sup>7:30</sup> |
| p.23 | 68 | je | dors <sup>sleep</sup> dans ma chambre <sup>bedroom</sup> |
| p.23 | 69 | je | viens <sup>come</sup> au collège à pied <sup>on foot</sup> [à vélo <sup>by bike</sup>] |
| p.24 | 70 | je | vois <sup>see</sup> mes cousins |
| p.24 | 71 | je | ne veux pas <sup>don't want</sup> ranger <sup>tidy</sup> mes affaires <sup>things (belongings)</sup> |

## Reflexive Verbs

| p.25 | 72 | je | m'amuse bien <sup>enjoy myself / have a good time</sup> |
|---|---|---|---|
| p.25 | 73 | je | me couche <sup>go to bed</sup> |
| p.25 | 74 | je | m'ennuie <sup>I'm bored</sup> |
| p.25 | 75 | je | m'entends bien <sup>get on well</sup> avec ma famille |
| p.25 | 76 | je | me lève <sup>get up</sup> |
| p.25 | 77 | je | me promène <sup>I go for a walk</sup> |
| p.25 | 78 | je | me repose <sup>rest</sup> |
| p.25 | 79 | je | me réveille <sup>wake up</sup> |

| 66 | I go out at the weekend | p.94 |
|---|---|---|
| 67 | I leave at 7:30 | p.96/ p.109 |
| 68 | I sleep in my bedroom | p.55 |
| 69 | I walk [I bike] to school | p.63/ p.107 |
| 70 | I see my cousins | p.55 |
| 71 | I don't want to tidy my things | p.48/ 49/55 |

## Reflexive Verbs

| 72 | I enjoy myself / have a good time | p.109 |
|---|---|---|
| 73 | I go to bed | |
| 74 | I am / get bored | p.15 |
| 75 | I get on well with my family | p.55 |
| 76 | I get up | p.16 |
| 77 | I (go for a) walk | p.16/ p.103 |
| 78 | I rest | |
| 79 | I wake up | |

## Passé composé Pages 26-33

Use the Perfect Tense for:  what you **did ONCE** in the **PAST**

The order of the -er verbs is the same as the list in the Present Tense on pp10-11 in FVMEplus.

| p.26 | 80 | j' | ai regardé la télé |
|---|---|---|---|
| p.26/ p.10 | 81 | j' | ai acheté ᵇᵒᵘᵍʰᵗ un appareil ᶜᵃᵐᵉʳᵃ |
| p.26/ p.10 | 82 | j' | ai apporté ᵇʳᵒᵘᵍʰᵗ mon maillot ˢʷⁱᵐˢᵘⁱᵗ |
| p.26/ p.10 | 83 | j' | ai attrapé ᶜᵃᵘᵍʰᵗ la balle |
| p.26/ p.10 | 84 | j' | ai bavardé ᶜʰᵃᵗᵗᵉᵈ avec mes amis |
| p.26/ p.10 | 85 | j' | ai cherché ˡᵒᵒᵏᵉᵈ ᶠᵒʳ mes chaussures ˢʰᵒᵉˢ |
| p.26/ p.10 | 86 | j' | ai commencé ˢᵗᵃʳᵗᵉᵈ à écrire ʷʳⁱᵗᵉ |
| p.26/ p.10 | 87 | j' | ai dépensé ˢᵖᵉⁿᵗ tout ᵃˡˡ mon argent ᵐᵒⁿᵉʸ |
| p.26/ p.10 | 88 | j' | ai deviné ᵍᵘᵉˢˢᵉᵈ la réponse ʳᵉᵖˡʸ |
| p.26/ p.10 | 89 | j' | ai donné ᵍᵃᵛᵉ un cadeau ᵖʳᵉˢᵉⁿᵗ à ma tante ᵃᵘⁿᵗ |
| p.26/ p.10 | 90 | j' | ai écouté ˡⁱˢᵗᵉⁿᵉᵈ ᵗᵒ le professeur |
| p.26/ p.10 | 91 | j' | ai envoyé ˢᵉⁿᵗ une lettre à |
| p.26/ p.10 | 92 | j' | ai gagné ʷᵒⁿ un prix ᵖʳⁱᶻᵉ |
| p.26/ p.11 | 93 | j' | ai invité mon cousin |

# Perfect Tense **Pages 26-33**

Use the Perfect Tense for:     what you **did ONCE** in the PAST

The order of the -er verbs is the same as the list in the Present Tense on pp10-11 in FVMEplus.

| | | |
|---|---|---|
| 80 | I watched TV | |
| 81 | I bought a camera | |
| 82 | I've brought my swimsuit | p.55 |
| 83 | I caught the ball | |
| 84 | I chatted with my friends | p.55 |
| 85 | I have looked for my shoes | p.55/ p.91 |
| 86 | I began to write | |
| 87 | I've spent all my money | p.77/ p.105 |
| 88 | I guessed the answer/reply | |
| 89 | I gave my aunt a present | p.55 |
| 90 | I listened to the teacher | p.91 |
| 91 | I sent a letter to… | p.15 |
| 92 | I won a prize | |
| 93 | I invited my cousin | p.55 |

# 16

| p.26/ p.11 | 94 | j' | ai joué aux échecs <sup>chess</sup> |
|---|---|---|---|
| p.26/ p.11 | 95 | j' | ai mangé une pomme |
| p.26/ p.11 | 96 | j' | ai nagé <sup>swam</sup> dans la mer |
| p.26/ p.11 | 97 | j' | ai oublié <sup>forgot</sup> mon portable <sup>mobile</sup> |
| p.26/ p.11 | 98 | j' | ai préparé le repas <sup>meal</sup> |
| p.26/ p.11 | 99 | j' | ai quitté <sup>left</sup> la gare |
| p.26/ p.11 | 100 | j' | ai remarqué <sup>noticed</sup> un agent <sup>policeman</sup> |
| p.26/ p.11 | 101 | j' | ai téléphoné à mon grand-père |
| p.26/ p.11 | 102 | j' | ai travaillé <sup>worked</sup> à la plage <sup>beach</sup> |
| p.26/ p.11 | 103 | j' | ai traversé <sup>crossed</sup> la place <sup>square</sup> |
| p.26/ p.11 | 104 | j' | ai trouvé <sup>found</sup> mon porte-monnaie <sup>purse</sup> |
| p.26/ p.11 | 105 | j' | ai vérifié <sup>checked</sup> les billets <sup>tickets</sup> |
| p.26/ p.11 | 106 | j' | ai voyagé <sup>travelled</sup> en Espagne <sup>Spain</sup> |
| p.27/ p.12 | 107 | j' | ai fini mon stage <sup>course / work experience</sup> |
| p.27/ p.12 | 108 | j' | ai choisi mon émission <sup>programme</sup> préférée |
| p.27/ p.12 | 109 | j' | ai rempli <sup>filled</sup> mon portefeuille <sup>wallet</sup> |
| p.27/ p.12 | 110 | j' | ai réussi <sup>passed</sup> à mon examen |
| p.27/ p.12 | 111 | j' | ai saisi <sup>grabbed</sup> mon blouson <sup>jacket</sup> |

| 94  | I played chess                 | p.102           |
|-----|--------------------------------|-----------------|
| 95  | I ate an apple                 |                 |
| 96  | I swam in the sea              |                 |
| 97  | I forgot my mobile             | p.55            |
| 98  | I prepared the meal            |                 |
| 99  | I left the station             | p.108           |
| 100 | I noticed a policeman          |                 |
| 101 | I phoned my grandfather        | p.55            |
| 102 | I worked on the beach          | p.64            |
| 103 | I crossed the square           |                 |
| 104 | I found my purse               | p.55            |
| 105 | I checked the tickets          |                 |
| 106 | I have travelled in Spain      | p.100/ p.106    |
| 107 | I finished my course           | p.55            |
| 108 | I chose my favourite programme | p.55/ p.70      |
| 109 | I filled my wallet             | p.55            |
| 110 | I passed my exam               | p.40/ p.55      |
| 111 | I grabbed my jacket            | p.55            |

| p.27/ p.13 | 112 | j' | ai vendu sold mon vieux old vélo |
| p.27/ p.13 | 113 | j' | ai attendu waited for le train |
| p.27/ p.13 | 114 | j' | ai entendu heard un bruit noise |
| p.27/ p.13 | 115 | j' | ai perdu lost mon passeport |
| p.28 | 116 | j' | ai pris caught/took le métro tube |
| p.28 | 117 | j' | ai appris learnt la leçon lesson |
| p.28 | 118 | j' | ai pris had un biftek-frites steak & chips |
| p.28 | 119 | j' | ai compris understood la carte map |
| p.28 | 120 | j' | ai mis put on mon imperméable raincoat |
| p.28 | 121 | j' | ai promis de faire make mon lit bed |
| p.28 | 122 | j' | ai fait did la vaisselle washing up |
| p.28 | 123 | j' | ai écrit wrote une carte postale postcard |
| p.28 | 124 | j' | ai dormi slept toute all la nuit night |
| p.28 | 125 | je | n'ai pas menti did not lie/tell a lie |
| p.29 | 126 | j' | ai été was surpris(e) |
| p.29 | 127 | j' | ai eu peur was afraid (literally: had fear) |
| p.29 | 128 | j' | ai bu drank du cidre |
| p.29 | 129 | j' | ai dû had to passer l'aspirateur vacuum |
| p.29 | 130 | j' | ai lu read le livre entier whole/entire |
| p.29 | 131 | j' | ai pu was able sortir to go out le weekend |
| p.29 | 132 | j' | ai vu saw un film épatant super |

| 112 | I sold my old bike | p.55/ p.77 |
| 113 | I waited for the train | p.91 |
| 114 | I heard a noise | |
| 115 | I (have) lost my passport | p.55 |
| 116 | I caught the tube | |
| 117 | I learnt the lesson | |
| 118 | I had a steak and chips | |
| 119 | I understood the map | |
| 120 | I put my raincoat on | p.55 |
| 121 | I promised to make my bed | p.55 |
| 122 | I did the washing up | |
| 123 | I wrote a postcard | |
| 124 | I slept all night | p.77 |
| 125 | I didn't tell a lie | p.50 |
| 126 | I was surprised | |
| 127 | I was afraid | p.86 |
| 128 | I drank (some) cider | p.67 |
| 129 | I had to do the vacuuming | |
| 130 | I read the whole book | p.75 |
| 131 | I was able to go out at the weekend | p.94 |
| 132 | I saw a super film | p.69 |

| p.29 | **133** | j' | ai couru <sup>ran</sup> vers <sup>towards</sup> la sortie <sup>exit</sup> |
|---|---|---|---|
| p.29 | **134** | j' | ai reçu <sup>received/got</sup> un joli <sup>pretty</sup> foulard <sup>scarf</sup> |
| p.29 | **135** | j' | ai tenu <sup>kept (held)</sup> ma promesse |
| p.29 | **136** | il | a fallu <sup>we had to</sup> partir <sup>leave</sup> tout de suite <sup>immediately</sup> |
| p.29 | **137** | il | a plu <sup>it rained</sup> hier <sup>yesterday</sup> |
| p.31 | **138** | je | suis allé(e) <sup>went</sup> à Paris |
| p.32 | **139** | je | suis arrivé(e) <sup>arrived</sup> en France |
| p.32 | **140** | je | suis monté(e) <sup>went up</sup> au sommet <sup>top</sup> de la Tour Eiffel |
| p.32 | **141** | je | suis rentré(e) <sup>got home</sup> à minuit <sup>midnight</sup> |
| p.32 | **142** | je | suis sorti(e) <sup>went out</sup> avec ma grand-mère |
| p.32 | **143** | je | suis parti(e) <sup>left</sup> à midi <sup>noon</sup> |
| p.32 | **144** | je | suis descendu(e) <sup>went down</sup> au rez-de-chaussée <sup>ground floor</sup> |
| p.32 | **145** | je | suis entré(e) <sup>went into</sup> dans la cour <sup>playground</sup> |
| p.32 | **146** | je | suis resté(e) <sup>stayed</sup> chez moi <sup>at home</sup> |

| 133 | I ran towards the exit | |
|-----|------------------------|--------|
| 134 | I got a pretty headscarf | p.70 |
| 135 | I kept my promise | p.55 |
| 136 | We had to leave immediately | p.109 |
| 137 | It rained yesterday | p.98 |
| 138 | I went to Paris | p.99 |
| 139 | I arrived in France | p.100 |
| 140 | I went up to the top of the Eiffel Tower | |
| 141 | I got home at midnight | p.96/ p.109 |
| 142 | I went out with my grandmother | p.55 |
| 143 | I left at noon/midday | p.96/ p.109 |
| 144 | I went down to the ground floor | p.63 |
| 145 | I went into the playground | p.106 |
| 146 | I stayed at home | p.62 |

# 22

## Verbes pronominaux (passé composé)

| | | | |
|---|---|---|---|
| p.33/ p.25 | **147** | je | me suis bien amusé(e) <sup>enjoyed myself/had a good time</sup> |
| p.33/ p.25 | **148** | je | me suis très bien amusé(e) <sup>had a very good time</sup> |
| p.33/ p.25 | **149** | je | ne me suis pas bien amusé(e) <sup>didn't enjoy myself</sup> |
| p.33/ p.25 | **150** | je | me suis brossé <sup>brushed</sup> les dents <sup>teeth</sup> |
| p.33/ p.25 | **151** | je | me suis couché(e) <sup>went to bed</sup> à 10 heures et demie <sup>10:30</sup> |
| p.33/ p.25 | **152** | je | me suis habillé(e) <sup>dressed</sup> |
| p.33/ p.25 | **153** | je | me suis lavé(e) <sup>washed</sup> |
| p.33/ p.25 | **154** | je | me suis levé(e) <sup>got up</sup> à 6 heures et quart <sup>6:15</sup> |
| p.33/ p.25 | **155** | je | me suis installé(e) <sup>settled down</sup> dans un fauteuil <sup>armchair</sup> |
| p.33/ p.25 | **156** | je | me suis reposé(e) <sup>rested</sup> |
| p.33/ p.25 | **157** | je | me suis réveillé(e) <sup>woke up</sup> à 6 heures |

# 23

## Reflexive Verbs (Perfect Tense)

| | | |
|---|---|---|
| 147 | I enjoyed myself / had a good time | p.109 |
| 148 | I had a very good time | p.109 |
| 149 | I didn't enjoy myself | p.109 |
| 150 | I brushed my teeth | |
| 151 | I went to bed at 10:30 | p.96 |
| 152 | I got dressed | |
| 153 | I washed | |
| 154 | I got up at 6:15 | p.96 |
| 155 | I settled down in an armchair | |
| 156 | I rested | |
| 157 | I woke up at 6 o'clock | p.96 |

## Imparfait Pages 34-35

Use the Imperfect Tense for:   What you **were doing**
What you **used to do**

| | | | |
|---|---|---|---|
| p.35 | 158 | quand j' | étais <sup>was</sup> petit(e) <sup>little</sup> |
| p.35 | 159 | quand j' | étais <sup>was</sup> jeune <sup>young</sup> |
| p.35 | 160 | quand j' | avais <u>was</u> 6 ans / 10 ans |
| p.10 | 161 | j' | aimais <sup>liked</sup> jouer au jardin |
| p.10 | 162 | je | dansais <sup>used to dance</sup> |
| p.10 | 163 | je | dessinais <sup>used to draw</sup> des bateaux <sup>boats</sup> |
| p.10/ p.34 | 164 | je | donnais <sup>used to give</sup> du pain aux oiseaux <sup>birds</sup> |
| p.10 | 165 | j' | écoutais <sup>used to listen to</sup> des disques <sup>records</sup> |
| p.11 | 166 | j' | habitais <sup>used to live</sup> à Manchester |
| p.11 | 167 | je | jouais <sup>used to play</sup> avec mon ballon <sup>ball</sup> / mes poupées <sup>dolls</sup> |
| p.35/ 17/11 | 168 | je | mangeais <sup>used to eat</sup> des bananes |
| p.11 | 169 | je | regardais <sup>used to watch</sup> des dessins animés <sup>cartoons</sup> |
| p.11 | 170 | je | tombais <sup>used to fall</sup> souvent <sup>often</sup> |
| p.11 | 171 | je | travaillais <sup>used to work</sup> pour mon oncle |

## Imperfect Tense  Pages 34-35

Use the Imperfect Tense for:   What you **were doing**

What you **used to do**

| 158 | When I was little | |
|---|---|---|
| 159 | When I was young | |
| 160 | When I was 6/10 | p.86 |
| 161 | I liked playing in the garden | |
| 162 | I used to dance | |
| 163 | I used to draw boats | |
| 164 | I used to give bread to the birds | p.64 |
| 165 | I used to listen to records | p.91 |
| 166 | I used to live in Manchester | p.99 |
| 167 | I used to play with my ball / dolls | |
| 168 | I used to eat bananas | p.17/ p.67 |
| 169 | I used to watch cartoons | |
| 170 | I often used to fall down | |
| 171 | I used to work for my uncle | p.55 |

| p.34/ p.12 | **172** | je | choisissais <sup>used to choose</sup> des bonbons <sup>sweets</sup> |
|---|---|---|---|
| p.34/ p.13 | **173** | je | perdais <sup>used to lose</sup> mes pantoufles <sup>slippers</sup> |
| p.34/ p.16 | **174** | j' | espérais <sup>hoped</sup> devenir <sup>to become</sup> mécanicien <sup>train driver</sup> |
| p.35/ p.19 | **175** | j' | allais <sup>used to go</sup> à l'école maternelle <sup>nursery school</sup> |
| p.19 | **176** | je | buvais <sup>used to drink</sup> beaucoup de lait <sup>milk</sup> |
| p.23 | **177** | je | dormais <sup>used to sleep</sup> l'après-midi <sup>afternoon</sup> |
| p.35/ p.21 | **178** | je | n'écrivais pas <sup>didn't write</sup> |
| p.21 | **179** | je | faisais <sup>made</sup> beaucoup de bruit <sup>noise</sup> |
| p.35/ p.22 | **180** | je | mettais <sup>used to put</sup> mes doigts <sup>fingers</sup> dans l'assiette <sup>plate</sup> |
| p.35/ p.22 | **181** | je | ne pouvais pas <sup>couldn't</sup> sortir <sup>go out</sup> seul <sup>alone</sup> |
| p.35/ p.22 | **182** | je | prenais <sup>used to take</sup> les jouets <sup>toys</sup> de ma sœur cadette <sup>younger sister</sup> |
| p.35/ p.23 | **183** | je | venais <sup>used to come</sup> voir <sup>to see</sup> les canards <sup>ducks</sup> |
| p.35/ p.24 | **184** | je | voulais <sup>wanted</sup> être <sup>to be</sup> infirmière <sup>nurse</sup> |
| p.35 | **185** | j' | étais <sup>was</sup> vendeur/vendeuse <sup>sales assistant</sup> |

You can easily change all of these to
**il** = he, **elle** = she, **on** = one/we   by changing the ending to **-ait**

| | | |
|---|---|---|
| 172 | I used to choose sweets | |
| 173 | I used to lose my slippers | p.55 |
| 174 | I hoped to become a train driver | p.23 |
| 175 | I used to go to nursery school | p.64 |
| 176 | I used to drink lots of milk | p.68 |
| 177 | I used to sleep in the afternoon | p.105 |
| 178 | I didn't write | p.48 |
| 179 | I made a lot of noise | p.68 |
| 180 | I used to put my fingers in the plate | |
| 181 | I couldn't go out alone | p.48 |
| 182 | I used to take my younger sister's toys | p.55 |
| 183 | I used to come and see the ducks | |
| 184 | I wanted to be nurse | |
| 185 | I was a sales assistant | |

You can easily change all of these to
   **il** = he, **elle** = she, **on** = one/we   by changing the ending to **-ait**

## Futur Simple  Pages 36-37

Use the Future Tense for:    What you **will do**

| | | | |
|---|---|---|---|
| p.36/ p.10 | 186 | je | donnerai <sup>will give</sup> ces fleurs |
| p.36/ p.10 | 187 | j' | accompagnerai <sup>will accompany</sup> la petite fille |
| p.36/ p.10 | 188 | j' | aiderai <sup>will help</sup> la vieille <sup>old</sup> dame <sup>lady</sup> |
| p.36/ p.10 | 189 | je | chercherai <sup>will look for</sup> une boîte aux lettres <sup>pillar box</sup> |
| p.36/ p.10 | 190 | j' | emprunterai <sup>will borrow</sup> un livre à <u>from</u> la bibliothèque <sup>library</sup> |
| p.36/ p.10 | 191 | je | garderai <sup>will look after</sup> des petits enfants |
| p.36/ p.10 | 192 | j' | habiterai <sup>will live</sup> aux Etats-Unis |
| p.36/ p.11 | 193 | j' | inviterai mes grands-parents |
| p.36/ p.11 | 194 | je | montrerai <sup>will show</sup> ce tableau <sup>this picture</sup> à notre voisin <sup>our neighbour</sup> |
| p.36/ p.11 | 195 | je | n'oublierai jamais <sup>will never forget</sup> ça <sup>that</sup> |
| p.36/ p.11 | 196 | je | passerai <sup>will spend</sup> un mois <sup>month</sup> en Allemagne <sup>Germany</sup> |
| p.36/ p.11 | 197 | je | porterai <sup>will wear</sup> mon meilleur <sup>best</sup> pullover |
| p.36/ p.11 | 198 | je | regarderai <sup>will watch</sup> le championnat <sup>championship</sup> |

## Future Tense  Pages 36-37

Use the Future Tense for:     What you **will do**

| 186 | I will give these flowers | p.55 |
|---|---|---|
| 187 | I will accompany the little girl | p.69 |
| 188 | I will help the old lady | p.77 |
| 189 | I will look for a pillar box | p.91 |
| 190 | I will borrow a book from the library | p.64 |
| 191 | I will look after small children | p.69 |
| 192 | I will live in the USA | p.101 |
| 193 | I will invite my grandparents | p.55 |
| 194 | I will show our neighbour this picture | p.55 |
| 195 | I will never forget that | p.48 |
| 196 | I will spend a month in Germany | p.100 |
| 197 | I will wear my best pullover | p.70/ p.55 |
| 198 | I will watch the championship | |

| | | | |
|---|---|---|---|
| p.36/<br>p.11 | **199** | je | rencontrerai <sup>will meet</sup> des gens <sup>people</sup> intéressants |
| p.36/<br>p.11 | **200** | je | travaillerai <sup>will work</sup> à l'étranger <sup>abroad</sup> |
| p.36/<br>p.11 | **201** | je | voyagerai <sup>will travel</sup> dans le monde entier <sup>over the whole world</sup> |
| p.36/<br>p.12 | **202** | je | finirai <sup>will finish</sup> mes études <sup>studies</sup> |
| p.36/<br>p.12 | **203** | je | choisirai <sup>will choose</sup> des sports de frisson <sup>extreme sports</sup> |
| p.36/<br>p.13 | **204** | j' | attendrai <sup>will wait for</sup> un bon poste <sup>good job</sup> |
| p.36/<br>p.23 | **205** | je | partirai en vacances <sup>will go on holiday</sup> |
| p.36/<br>p.23 | **206** | je | sortirai <sup>will go out</sup> avec mon équipe <sup>team</sup> |
| p.36/<br>p.19 | **207** | je | boirai <sup>will drink</sup> un verre <sup>glass</sup> de vin |
| p.36/<br>p.22 | **208** | je | mettrai <sup>will put</sup> le poulet au four <sup>oven</sup> |
| p.36/<br>p.22 | **209** | je | prendrai <sup>will take</sup> de belles photos <sup>some fine photos</sup> |

| 199 | I will meet interesting people | p.108/ p.70 |
|---|---|---|
| 200 | I will work abroad | p.64 |
| 201 | I will travel over the whole world | p.75 |
| 202 | I will finish my studies | p.55 |
| 203 | I will choose extreme sports | p.103 |
| 204 | I will wait for a good job | p.91 |
| 205 | I will go on holiday | p.108 |
| 206 | I will go out with my team | p.55 |
| 207 | I will drink a glass of wine | p.68 |
| 208 | I will put the chicken in the oven | |
| 209 | I will take some fine photos | p.77 |

## 32

| p.37 | 210 | | je | serai will be avocat a lawyer |
| p.37 | 211 | | j' | aurai will have un appartement flat en ville |
| p.37 | 212 | | j' | irai will go à l'université |
| p.37 | 213 | | je | ferai des randonnées will do/go on hikes |
| p.37 | 214 | | je | devrai will have to réussir pass à mes examens my exams |
| p.37 | 215 | | je | pourrai shall be able payer to pay for des excursions |
| p.37 | 216 | | je | verrai will see une pièce de théâtre play |
| p.37 | 217 | | je | viendrai shall come souvent often chez mes parents to my parents' house |
| p.37 | 218 | | j' | achèterai will buy une auto car |
| p.37 | 219 | quand j' | aurai am (literally: will be) 18 ans |

**Conditional Tense**

Add "s" to the Future "je" Verb form and translate "would"

*Eg:* j'irais = I would go

# La Fin

| 210 | I will be a lawyer | |
| 211 | I will have a flat in town | |
| 212 | I will go to university | p.64 |
| 213 | I will go on hikes | p.103 |
| 214 | I will have to pass my exams | p.55 |
| 215 | I shall be able to pay for outings | p.91 |
| 216 | I will see a play | p.106 |
| 217 | I shall often come to my parents' house | |
| 218 | I will buy a car | p.16 |
| 219 | When I'm 18 | p.86 |

**Conditional Tense**

Add "s" to the Future "je" Verb form and translate "would"

*Eg:* j'irais = I would go

# The End

Made in the USA
Las Vegas, NV
31 October 2021